The United States Constitution

KAREN PRICE HOSSELL

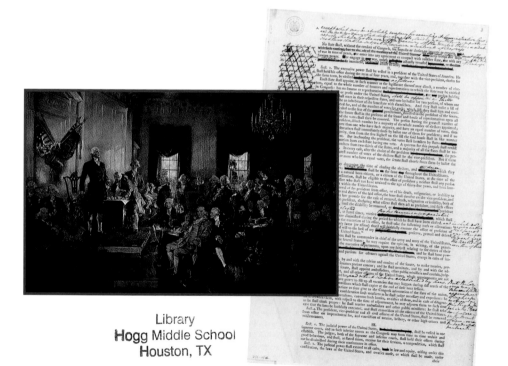

Heinemann Library
Chicago, Illinois

Designed by Herman Adler Design
Photo research by Bill Broyles
Printed and bound in the United States by Lake Book
Manufacturing, Inc.

08 07 06 05 04
10 9 8 7 6 5 4 3 2

Library of Congress Cataloging-in-Publication Data
Price Hossell, Karen, 1957-
   The United States Constitution / Karen Price Hossell.
      p. cm. -- (Historical documents)
Summary: Provides a history of the Constitution, explains
each section including the Bill of Rights and subsequent
amendments, and describes how historical documents such as
this can be restored and preserved.
Includes bibliographical references and index.
   ISBN 1-4034-0804-1 (hardcover) -- ISBN 1-4034-3434-4
(pbk.) 1. Constitutional history--United States--Juvenile
literature. [1. Constitutional history--United States.] I. Title.
II. Historical documents (Heinemann Library (Firm))
   KF4550.Z9P69 2003
   342.73'029--dc21
                                       2003008196

Acknowledgments
The author and publisher are grateful to the following for
permission to reproduce copyright material:

Cover photographs by (document) National Archives and
Records Administration, (portraits, t-b) Bettmann/Corbis,
The Corcoran Gallery of Art/Corbis, North Carolina
Museum of Art/Corbis; (title bar) Corbis.

Title page (L-R) Art Resource, NY, Library of Congress;
pp. 4, 24, 30, 32, 33, 34, 41, 42, 43, 44 National Archives
and Records Administration; pp. 6, 13t Lee Snider/Corbis; p. 7
Steve Deslich/KRT; pp. 8, 11 Hector Emanuel/Heinemann
Library; p. 9 Art Resource, NY; p. 10 Archivo Iconografico,
S. A./Corbis; pp. 12, 15, 18l, 20, 21, 29 North Wind Picture
Archives; p. 13b Réunion des Musées Nationaux/Art
Resource, NY; p. 16 The Historical Society of Pennsylvania;
p. 17 Hulton Archive/Getty Images; p. 18r Stapleton
Collection/Corbis; pp. 22, 28, 36, 37, Library of Congress;
pp. 23, 39 Bettmann/Corbis; p. 25 Joseph Sohm/
ChromoSohm Inc./Corbis; p. 26 North Carolina Museum
of Art/Corbis; p. 27 Independence National Historical Park;
pp. 31, 38 Corbis; p. 35 Mario Tama/Getty Images; p. 40
Stock Montage, Inc.; p. 45 Richard T. Nowitz/Corbis.

Every effort has been made to contact copyright holders
of any material reproduced in this book. Any omissions will
be rectified in subsequent printings if notice is given to the
publisher.

Some words are shown in bold, **like
this.** You can find out what they mean
by looking in the glossary.

Contents

Recording Important Events

Throughout history, people have created documents so they will have a record of an important event. Documents may reveal how people lived, how major discoveries were made, or what occurred during a war.

Documents that provide a historical record of something can be divided into two groups: **primary sources** and **secondary sources.**

Primary sources

When historians are studying what happened in the past, they prefer to use primary sources. This term refers to documents that provide a firsthand account of an event. Primary sources can include letters, diaries, newspaper articles, **pamphlets,** and other papers that were written by people who witnessed or were directly involved in an event.

Primary sources can also include official papers that were carefully planned, often with much discussion and argument. The people involved in the planning and writing of

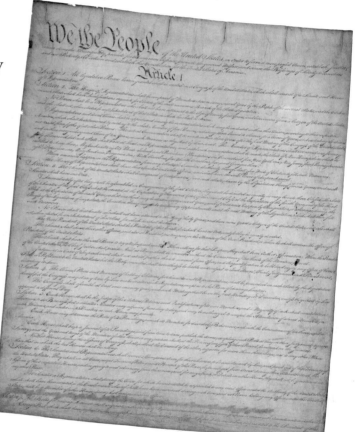

The Constitution is an important primary source of United States history.

these papers were careful to make sure the words in the documents expressed the exact thoughts and ideas they wanted them to. Official papers are usually a clear record of just what the authors intended to say.

The original thirteen colonies declared independence from Great Britain in 1776. With this new found freedom, Americans had to create their own government.

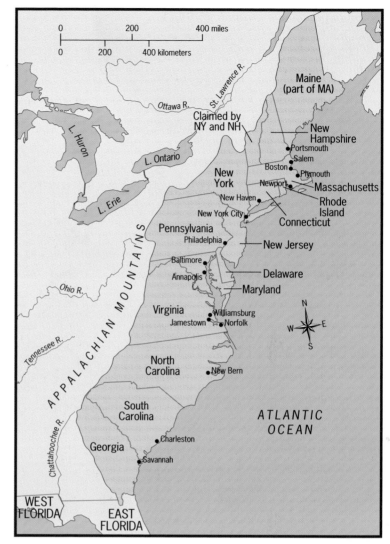

Primary sources tell us, in the words of the people who lived during that time, what really happened. They are a kind of direct communication that has not been filtered through a lot of other sources. Often, stories that are passed verbally from person to person change as they are told and retold. Facts become muddled and confused, and information is added or left out. Over time, facts are changed or twisted, either accidentally or on purpose, and the original story has completely changed. As a result, unwritten accounts of what happened in the past are often incorrect. To find out what really happened and why, historians rely on printed or handwritten primary sources.

Secondary sources

Secondary sources are accounts of events written by people who have studied primary sources. They read letters, **journals,** and other firsthand accounts, then write their own version based on their research.

Storing Valuable Documents

Because **primary sources** provide an important record of historical events, they are considered valuable. For that reason, the paper-and-ink documents are carefully handled and stored so that they will last a long time.

Documents that are considered valuable records of United States history are kept in several different places. The two institutions that hold most of these historical records are the Library of Congress and the National Archives and Records Administration, or NARA.

The Library of Congress

The Library of Congress is in Washington, D.C. It is a **federal** institution and also the largest library in the world. The library holds about 120 million items, including maps, books, and photographs. Its collection is available to members of **Congress,** as well as to the rest of the American public.

In the winter, visitors can ice-skate in front of the NARA in Washington, D.C.

Archivist Rick Blondo examines files in the stacks at the NARA. He was involved in the recent renovation of the archives, which reopened to visitors on September 17, 2003.

The NARA

The NARA is another government agency. It manages all federal records. Besides paper documents, the NARA also holds films, photographs, posters, sound and video recordings, and other types of government records. The original documents in the NARA collection provide a history of the U.S. government. They also tell the story of American settlement, industry, and farming. In fact, documents and other **artifacts** detailing almost every aspect of American history can be found in the NARA collection.

Most of the documents at the NARA are stored in specially designed boxes. Since paper is made from plants, it contains acids. Over time, these acids can discolor paper, turning it so dark that the ink on it cannot be read. For this reason, NARA storage boxes are acid-free. The boxes are stored in fireproof, locked **stacks** at the NARA's 41 different facilities. The temperature and **humidity** in NARA storage areas are carefully controlled, because heat and humidity can **deteriorate** documents.

What Is the Constitution?

The Constitution is one of the most important documents in the United States. It lays out the **foundation** for the nation's government.

Background

To understand how the Constitution came to be, one has to go back to 1776. In the spring of that year, the founders of the United States were writing the **Declaration of Independence.** At the same time, they were also forming a new government for the country. That new government was called a **confederation,** and its ruling document was the Articles of Confederation. From 1781 to 1789, the United States government operated under these Articles.

Many leaders, however, were unhappy with this government. Instead of being a strong, unified confederacy, the United States was becoming weak. In fact, leaders of some European countries were tracking the problems the young country was having. They believed that if they waited long enough, the confederation would break down completely. Then they could come in and take over.

The Constitutional Convention

In 1787, political leaders decided they should meet to discuss ways to change the Articles of Confederation. They met at Independence Hall in Philadelphia, Pennsylvania, in the same room where the

Independence Hall in Philadelphia, Pennsylvania, was the site of many important meetings in U.S. history.

Often, the meetings of the Constitutional Convention followed strict rules of conduct, to make sure that everyone's opinion was heard.

Declaration of Independence was signed. This meeting is known as the Constitutional Convention. At the convention, leaders **drafted** a new governing document called the Constitution.

A great experiment

The Constitution outlines a great experiment—the United States of America. In 1787, when the Constitution was written, the United States was only eleven years old. It was founded on the ideas of freedom and equality. The United States would not have rulers that got their position because they belonged to a particular family or had a great deal of wealth. Instead, leaders would be elected by the people of the nation. In those days, this was an unusual idea. That is why the United States was a kind of experiment.

A New Government

The **delegates** sent to the Constitutional Convention had been appointed by the **legislatures** of their states. Fifty-five delegates attended the Convention, but rarely all at once. Some members came and went. Rhode Island did not send delegates.

As the Constitutional Convention began, its members selected George Washington to be its president. They had great respect for Washington. As **commander-in-chief** of the Continental Army during the **Revolutionary War,** Washington had led the country to victory over the British. William Jackson, who had been a major in the war, was named as secretary.

George Washington was a well-respected leader in the United States.

A Constitution

In the first few days of the convention, delegates decided not to **revise** the Articles of **Confederation.** Instead, they voted to write a new document outlining a different kind of government. The document would be a constitution like the ones the states had been writing for themselves as they formed their own strong governments.

Know It

William Jackson served as secretary under George Washington twice. Jackson was secretary of the Constitutional Convention under Washington as Convention president. He was also Washington's personal secretary from 1789 to 1791, while Washington was president of the United States.

Fear of a federal government

Not all of the delegates agreed that the convention should write a new constitution. This was because some of them, representing the feelings of their legislatures, feared a strong central government. The states had agreed to the Articles of Confederation earlier for this very reason—it gave the states more power than it gave the general government. Now, these delegates feared that state powers would be taken away and given to a **federal** government. Some of them even walked out on the convention in disgust.

The Constitution Convention met in the Assembly Room at Independence Hall, also known as the Philadelphia State House. The room has been **restored** to the way it looked in 1787.

The Virginia Plan

Those who were against the idea of forming a strong central government were called anti-**federalists.** Those who wanted this kind of government were called federalists. Among the federalists were future presidents George Washington and James Madison, who were both from Virginia. The federalists wanted to strengthen the bond between the states and make them one firm **union.**

All of the Virginia **delegates** were federalists. They arrived early for the Constitutional Convention in Philadelphia. While they waited for the other delegates to arrive, they met and **drafted** a document called the Virginia Plan. James Madison is credited with writing most of the plan. On May 25, 1787, after most of the other delegates had arrived, the Constitutional Convention began. On May 29, Edmund Randolph, Virginia's governor, stood up and read the Virginia Plan.

Edmund Randolph

Three branches of government

The plan provided for three branches of government: **legislative, executive,** and **judicial.** The three branches represented a separation of powers. That means that no one branch would have all the power.

The legislative branch—the lawmaking part of government—would be made up of two houses, or sections. Members of one house would be elected by the people. Members of the other house would be elected by the first house. The executive branch would be made up of a national executive chosen by the **legislature.** Once elected, the executive could then name others to assist him. The judiciary branch would be headed by the **Supreme Court** and would also include minor courts under its influence.

Anti-federalists unhappy

Anti-federalists were not happy with the Virginia Plan. The idea of two houses of legislature was a new one in 1787. A government with one executive reminded them of England with its king. Plus, anti-federalists did not like the idea of a strong national government that could make laws for the states and force its **citizens** to pay taxes.

It was difficult for these men to understand the kind of government described in the Virginia Plan. No other country in the world had such a government, so there was no model for them to look at as they considered it.

After long meetings, delegates often went to the City Tavern of Philadelphia to have a drink and discuss the events of the day.

James Madison

In 1809, James Madison became the fourth president of the United States. It was Madison who drafted most of the Virginia Plan. Historians often call Madison the father of the Constitution, because the U.S. Constitution is based on his plan. He thought the United States needed a strong national government and worked to convince others of that need. Madison kept a diary and took many notes on what happened in convention meetings. In 1837, **Congress** bought the **journal** Madison kept during the convention. In fact, most of what we know today about the details of the Constitutional Convention comes from this important **primary source.**

The Delegates Debate

On May 29, 1787, the committee made up of all the **delegates** of the convention voted to have a national government with three branches, as described in the Virginia Plan. Then the delegates went through all the **resolutions** in the Virginia Plan and voted on each one. Sometimes they postponed the votes, intending to go back to those issues later and discuss them at length.

Delegates worked six days a week, with Sundays off. Often, the weather was hot. But no matter how hot it was, the doors and windows of the meeting room remained closed. The delegates did not want anyone to be able to stand outside a door or window and spy on the meetings.

Know It

In 1787, women had little or no place in government. They were not even allowed to vote! That is why you do not see the names of any women mentioned as convention delegates, and why the national executive is referred to as "him."

Debated issues

Some long **debates** took place that summer. One issue the delegates spent a lot of time with was the idea of a national **executive.** Some said this sounded too much like a king.

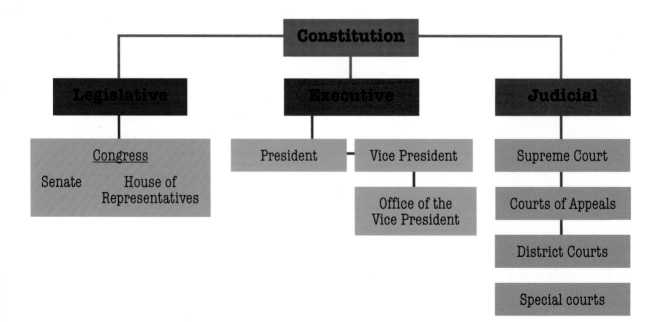

Constitution

Legislative — Congress — Senate, House of Representatives

Executive — President, Vice President — Office of the Vice President

Judicial — Supreme Court, Courts of Appeals, District Courts, Special courts

Sworn to secrecy

Delegates to the Constitutional Convention had to swear not to discuss their meetings with anyone except other delegates. They also promised to not let anyone see the notes they took. The official record of the convention—in the form of a **journal**—could be shown only to convention members. No member was allowed to copy from the journal, and nothing about the convention could be published in newspapers while the meetings were going on.

One reason the delegates were so secretive was that they wanted to appear united. They did not want to reveal any arguments that took place—or even that there were arguments at all. Also, they wanted to be able to change their minds about issues later.

Others wanted three executives— one for each branch of government. Delegates also discussed how much this person should be paid and who should be involved in electing him.

Perhaps the most debated issue had to do with the two **legislative** branches. The first branch was called the House of Representatives. Some convention members thought it would be better for state **legislatures** to choose the members. They believed that the people should not

The meetings of the Constitutional Convention were kept secret until 1819, when the journals of its meetings were published.

be given that much power. Others, though, thought that at least one branch of government should be elected by the people. After much discussion, members voted that the people should elect the representatives.

The First Draft

Another issue the convention **delegates debated** at length was how the states should be represented in the national **legislature.** Some thought there should be one representative for a certain number of people, such as one per 40,000. This is called **proportional representation.** Delegates from Delaware, New Jersey, New York, Maryland, Connecticut, and New Hampshire did not agree. These six states had smaller populations than the other seven. Delegates from these states thought that each state should have the same number of votes, no matter how many people lived there. Otherwise, they believed that the states with large populations, which under this system would have more representatives in **Congress,** would overrule the smaller ones, or even take them over.

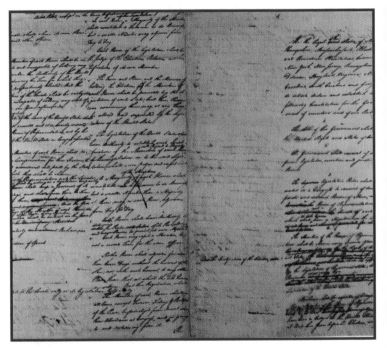

This first page of the first **draft** of the Constitution was written by Pennsylvania delegate James Wilson in August 1787. It is the earliest surviving version of the Constitution.

How the Convention was run

At the Constitutional Convention, the members ran the meetings in two different ways. When they met as a convention, they followed the formal rules of **parliamentary procedure** that were commonly used in such meetings. Delegates also met as a Committee of the Whole. This meant that they did not have to follow parliamentary procedure and could share opinions and information informally. When they wanted to make official votes, they declared that the convention was in session.

A compromise

Finally, Roger Sherman of Connecticut offered a **compromise**. He thought that one **legislative** house could have proportional representation. In the other house, each state would get one vote. The members agreed. They decided that the House of Representatives would have proportional representation, and the people would elect the representatives. The number of people to be represented would include all free white **citizens**—specifically, men—as well as three-fifths of the slave population.

Roger Sherman

Nineteen resolutions

On June 13, 1787, after all the issues had been discussed and voted on, the first draft of the Constitution was ready. The **chairman** of the committee, Nathaniel Gorham from Massachusetts, stood up and read the nineteen **resolutions** the members had discussed and voted on. Then he put the draft on a table so the delegates could copy from it and take the copy home to examine. The next day, they would vote on whether to **adopt** all of the nineteen resolutions.

The New Jersey Plan

On June 14, the delegates from New Jersey announced that they needed more time. They wanted to come up with another plan. They said that they were concerned about the direction the meeting was taking. The people who had sent them to the convention told them to **revise** the Articles of **Confederation,** not to write a new constitution. On June 16, New Jersey presented its plan, but it was voted down.

Working Out the Details

The **delegates** spent many more weeks working out the details of the Constitution. They decided how many years would make up the **terms** of **senators** and representatives, how they would be paid, and exactly how state representation would be determined. Delegates also figured out how the other branches of government would work as well.

The Committee of Detail

On July 26, 1787, all of the materials from the convention were given to a Committee of Detail. The members of this committee were John Rutledge of South Carolina, Edmund Randolph of Virginia, Nathaniel Gorham of Massachusetts, Oliver Ellsworth of Connecticut, and James Wilson of Pennsylvania. By that time, the convention had passed 23 **resolutions.** The committee was ordered to read the convention material, organize it, and rewrite it in clear language. They were told to complete the job in eleven days. While they worked, the rest of the delegates took some time off. The convention was **adjourned** until August 6.

John Rutledge

Oliver Ellsworth

The Committee's report

When the Committee of Detail finished its work, the members had 60 copies of the **revised** Virginia Plan printed. The printers, John Dunlap and David C. Claypoole of Philadelphia, Pennsylvania, were told to keep the job a secret. About sixteen of these copies are known to exist today. The Library of Congress has five copies, including one that belonged to James Madison. The NARA has two copies, including George Washington's copy. The remaining copies are at various libraries, historical societies, and in private collections around the United States.

On August 6, 1787, John Rutledge presented the committee's official second **draft** of the Virginia Plan (soon to be called the Constitution). The committee had written a **preamble**—an introductory paragraph— then listed the 23 articles. After the draft was presented, the meeting was again adjourned so everyone could read it.

Universal confidence

Because the meetings of the Constitutional Convention were kept secret, journalists and others who were interested looked for clues that would help them determine how the convention was going. This paragraph was published in a newspaper in Philadelphia called the *Pennsylvania Packet and Daily Advertiser* on August 23, 1787. It shows that writers had little to go on, except what they observed by standing outside Independence Hall.

The punctuality [promptness] with which the members of the Convention assemble every day at a certain hour, and the long time they spend in the deliberations [meetings] of each day (sometimes 7 hours) are proofs, among other things how much they are entitled to the universal confidence of the people of America. Such a body of enlightened [intelligent] and honest men perhaps never before met for the political purposes in any country upon the face of the earth.

The Committee of Style

On August 7, 1787, the **delegates** returned to Independence Hall with their second **draft** copies. Together, they carefully went over every section of the document, sometimes discussing each word that was used.

Their review of the draft took several weeks, and they **revised** entire sections of it. By September 8, the delegates decided they were finished, and that the next draft of what would become the United States Constitution was ready to be completed. They selected a Committee of Style to make the new changes. Officially, this committee was told "to revise the stile [style] and arrange the articles which had been agreed to by the House." The members of this committee were William Samuel Johnson of Connecticut, Alexander Hamilton of New York, Gouverneur Morris of Pennsylvania, James Madison of Virginia, and Rufus King of Massachusetts.

The Constitutional Convention opened with three major presentations, including the Hamilton Plan, presented by its 32-year-old author in a five hour long speech—the longest of the Convention.

Rufus King

Gouverneur Morris

Gouverneur Morris is credited with the wording of the Constitution. Morris was born in New York to a wealthy family. He studied to be a lawyer and soon became interested in politics. At the Constitutional Convention, he made at least 173 speeches—more than anyone else. After the convention he traveled to Europe, where he stayed for ten years. His close friend, President George Washington, made Morris minister to France in 1791. He died in 1816.

The Committee completes its work

By September 12, the Committee of Style had completed its task. The committee had taken the 23 articles from the second draft and simplified them so that this new version—the third draft—had only seven articles.

The convention ordered the committee to have 60 copies of its work printed. Of the copies, about fourteen are known to exist today. Many of these copies include notes written by the delegate who owned the copy.

The committee had also written a letter that would go along with the Constitution when it was presented to the Continental **Congress**. Printed copies of the letter were not made. It was read aloud to the convention, though, and they voted to agree to the entire letter.

Congress Approves
the Constitution

After they agreed to the letter, the **delegates** reviewed the new version of the Constitution, going over it in detail again. By this time, most of the delegates were very tired. They had been working hard for weeks, sitting in long meetings and listening to countless speeches as each delegate presented his opinion on issues. Now, they were ready to go home.

This printed version of the Constitution belonged to George Washington. He wrote notes in the margins on September 12, 1787.

Some unhappy delegates

As many delegates began to prepare for their journey home, some began to speak out against the final version of the Constitution. One of the delegates shocked many when, on Saturday, September 15, 1787, he stood up to speak. He said that he thought the document gave too much power to **Congress,** and that he was not comfortable with what had been written. The man in question was Edmund Randolph, who had presented the Virginia Plan to the convention!

Another Virginia delegate, George Mason, also expressed dissatisfaction. Mason had written the Virginia state constitution, which contained a **bill of rights.** He said that the U.S. Constitution should also have a bill of rights.

The delegates listened, but the majority voted to **adopt** the Constitution. The Convention then ordered the Constitution to be **engrossed,** which means to be handwritten in fancy writing, called calligraphy, on an expensive writing material called parchment.

George Mason had originally retired from politics in 1780. However, he did not stay retired for long, as his friends in politics still sought his advice and opinions on matters. Mason officially returned to politics during the **debate** to **revise** the Articles of **Confederation** seven years later, in 1787.

Engrossing the Document

The man who **engrossed** the Constitution was Jacob Shallus of Philadelphia, Pennsylvania. Shallus had fought in the **Revolutionary War** and was a clerk for the Pennsylvania **legislature.** The Convention paid him $30—a large sum—to do the job.

Parchment

Parchment is made from animal skin, usually the skin of a sheep, calf, or goat. All fur or hair is stripped or scraped from the skin. Then the skin is stretched on a frame and scraped some more.

Know It

For many years, historians were not sure whether Shallus engrossed the Constitution. They thought he probably did because he was a clerk for the Pennsylvania legislature, which met in Independence Hall, the same place the Convention was held. In 1937, handwriting **analysts** compared documents they knew had been engrossed by Shallus with the handwriting on the U.S. Constitution. They determined that he was indeed its engrosser.

The errata paragraph

Jacob Shallus did not have much time to engross the Constitution. He was given a copy of the document on September 15, 1787, and had to have the engrossed sheets ready by September 17, the following Monday. Since he had to work so quickly, he made some errors. On the last page of the document, after the final article, he wrote a paragraph stating the errors he had made. This is called an errata paragraph.

As the skin dries, it becomes strong, like a thin piece of leather. Parchment was expensive, but it was made to last a long time. When a document was sent to be engrossed, it indicated that those in charge of the document considered it to be in its final form. The Constitution took up four sheets of parchment. Each of the sheets is 28 inches (71 centimeters) long by 23 5/8 inches (60 centimeters) wide.

The tools he used

Engrossers like Shallus wrote in large letters using fancy writing called calligraphy. They used quill pens made from goose, duck, swan, or pheasant feathers. Each pen was cut to a point and dipped into an inkwell. Some of the ink rose into the hollow quill, so the writer could write several words before dipping the quill into the ink again. The ink used to write the engrossed copy of the Constitution was iron-gall ink, made from oak trees and several kinds of dye.

While the engrosser wrote, he spread a light coat of finely powdered **pumice** over the surface of the parchment. This was to keep the ink from feathering, or spreading.

To make sure that his lines were straight, Shallus made guidelines on the parchment with pale brown crayon. Those lines are still visible today. To remove mistakes, engrossers sometimes scraped away the ink with a penknife.

The *Rising Sun* chair served as George Washington's seat at the Constitutional Convention. It is still located in Independence Hall, where the Convention took place in 1787. The quill and inkpot are similar to what the **delegates** would have used.

The Final Document

On September 17, 1787, Benjamin Franklin made a **motion** that the **delegates** sign the Constitution. The motion passed, so 39 delegates signed the document in geographical order, starting in the north with New Hampshire and working south to Georgia. After the document was signed, the convention was **adjourned.**

Destroying the notes

Many historians regret what happened later that afternoon. The secretary of the convention, William Jackson, was ordered to burn all of the notes and other papers that came out of the convention—important **primary sources.** The delegates wanted him to

Benjamin Franklin was the oldest delegate at the Constitutional Convention.

do this for many reasons. First, they did not want a public record of how strongly they had disagreed over certain issues. Second, they also did not want the public to read about some of the things they had originally wanted to include in the Constitution, and later changed their minds and removed. Finally, the delegates wanted the final four-page document to stand alone.

Refusing to sign

Three men refused to add their signatures to the Constitution. They were Elbridge Gerry, Edmund Randolph, and George Mason. These men feared that the **federal** government established by the Constitution might be too powerful. In addition, they were disappointed that the document did not contain a **bill of rights.**

Making the Constitution public

Besides the **engrossed** version, other copies of the Constitution were produced on the weekend of September 15. Printers Dunlap and Claypoole were hired to make 500 copies of the Constitution. The delegates would bring these copies to their various states, where they would be handed out at the state **legislatures.**

Today, seven of these copies are in various libraries and other collections. One copy is at Independence National Historical Park in Philadelphia, Pennsylvania, also known as Independence Hall.

On September 18, William Jackson carried the Constitution to the Continental **Congress** in New York City. The first printing for the public took place on September 19. It is not known exactly how many copies were made, but eighteen of them exist today.

On September 20, 1787, the Constitution was read aloud in Congress. Congress **debated** for several days whether to present the document to the states for **ratification.** On September 29, they voted to do so.

Know It

Besides the Constitution, Roger Sherman of Connecticut also signed the **Declaration of Independence** and the Articles of **Confederation.** He is the only man to have signed all three documents.

This inkstand was used to sign the Declaration of Independence. Something similar would have been used to sign the Constitution.

Ratification

Even before **Congress** had seen the Constitution, it became known to the public. As soon as newspapers had copies of the document, they published it for their readers.

The Constitution also became known through the Constitutional Convention **delegates.** The delegates shared their copies, mailing them to friends and acquaintances and showing them to dinner guests. Benjamin Franklin and George Washington sometimes included copies of the Constitution in their letters. Along with the printed copies, delegates sent messages urging those who received the document to **ratify** it.

A push for ratification

Three political leaders of the time found yet another way to gain support for ratification. Alexander Hamilton, James Madison, and John Jay began to write essays that were published in New York newspapers. The essays focused on the need for a strong **federal** government and were written to encourage ratification in New York, which had a powerful anti-**federalist**

Know It

After his involvement in the Constitutional Convention, John Jay later became the first **chief justice** of the United States **Supreme Court.**

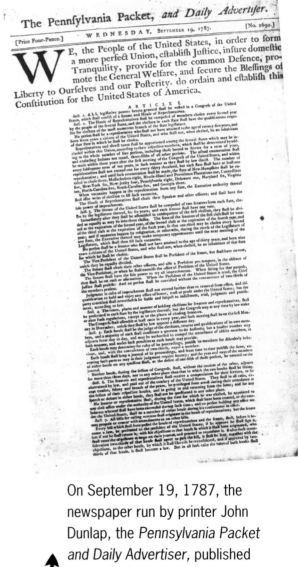

On September 19, 1787, the newspaper run by printer John Dunlap, the *Pennsylvania Packet and Daily Advertiser*, published the Constitution.

force that included the governor. Later, these essays were published in a book called *The Federalist Papers*.

Debates over ratification

As the content of the Constitution became known, federalists and anti-federalists began to speak out for or against it. State ratification conventions were sites of heated **debates** between those who wanted a government like that described in the Constitution, and those who preferred power to remain with the states.

The Constitution becomes official

The members of the Constitutional Convention had decided that nine states had to ratify the Constitution in order for it to become the official governing document of the United States. By June 21, 1788, Delaware, Pennsylvania, New Jersey, Georgia, Connecticut, Massachusetts, Maryland, South Carolina, and New Hampshire had approved the Constitution. It was now official.

THE

FEDERALIST:

ADDRESSED TO THE

PEOPLE OF THE STATE OF NEW-YORK.

NUMBER I.

Introduction.

AFTER an unequivocal experience of the inefficacy of the subsisting federal government, you are called upon to deliberate on a new constitution for the United States of America. The subject speaks its own importance; comprehending in its consequences, nothing less than the existence of the UNION, the safety and welfare of the parts of which it is composed, the fate of an empire, in many respects, the most interesting in the world. It has been frequently remarked, that it seems to have been reserved to the people of this country, by their conduct and example, to decide the important question, whether societies of men are really capable or not, of establishing good government from reflection and choice, or whether they are forever destined to depend, for their political constitutions, on accident and force. If there be any truth in the remark, the crisis, at which we are arrived, may with propriety be regarded as the æra in which

A   that

Hamilton, Madison, and Jay did not sign their names to their essays. Instead, they signed each essay "Publius." Basically, the men wanted readers to know that the essays were written by the people, for the people.

Once nine states had ratified the Constitution, Congress began setting up the new government. On August 6, 1788, it instructed states to start electing representatives for the federal **legislature.** On March 4, 1789, the new government began operation. On April 30, 1789, George Washington became the nation's first president. All three branches of government began to function with the first session of the Supreme Court on February 2, 1790.

The Preamble and Articles I, II, III

The Constitution contains seven articles. Some of the articles are broken up into smaller parts, called sections.

The preamble

The first paragraph of the Constitution is called the **preamble.** In the preamble, the writers of the Constitution explain what they hoped to accomplish by creating the document. It says:

We the people of the United States, in Order to form a more perfect **Union,** *establish Justice, insure domestic Tranquility* [peace], *provide for the common defence, promote the general Welfare, and secure the Blessings of Liberty to ourselves and our Posterity* [future generations], *do ordain* [order by law] *and establish the Constitution for the United States of America.*

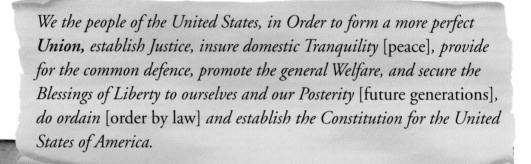

The first three articles

The first three articles of the Constitution describe the powers of the three branches of government—**legislative, executive,** and **judicial.** Article I outlines the legislative powers of the government. Those powers are given to **Congress,** which is made up of two parts, a Senate and a House of Representatives. The article goes on to explain the qualifications of members of the House and Senate, including how long their **terms** will be, how old they must be to be elected, how they will be elected, and other details. The Article also describes the powers of Congress, listing what it can and cannot do.

Article II discusses the nation's executive, the President of the United States. It explains how long the president's term should be, how the election should be held, who is qualified to become president, and the powers and duties of the president.

Article III describes the judiciary. It is made up of the most powerful court in the United States, the **Supreme Court,** as well as minor courts under its influence. The article lists the powers of this court system and directs how trials should be conducted.

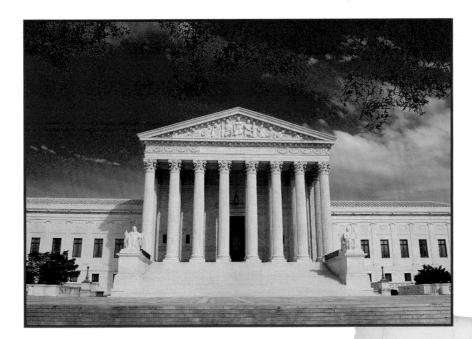

The U.S. Supreme Court Building was built from 1932 to 1935 in Washington, D.C. The first session of the Supreme Court occurred on February 1, 1790. It only took 145 years for the Supreme Court to find a permanent home!

Articles IV–V

Article IV of the Constitution discusses the states in four sections. It explains that each state should respect the laws and decisions of the other states. The first section says that **Congress** has the power to make laws about the public acts, records, and **judicial** proceedings of the states. The second section says that the **citizens** of all the states have the same rights and privileges. Also, if a person commits a crime in one state and then flees to another state, he or she can be forced to return to the state in which the crime was committed.

The states

Section 3 describes how new states can be formed. Congress has power over new territories—that is, U.S. land that is not yet a state—and any other property the United States owns. Section 4 guarantees each state a **republican** form of government, as well as ensuring the protection of the states against invasion or other forms of violence.

Amendments

Article V describes how **amendments** can be added to the Constitution. The writers of the Constitution knew that the best **foundation** for government was one that allowed for change. For this reason, they included two procedures in the Constitution that provided for amendments, or changes, to the document. The first way is for two-thirds of the members of both the House of Representatives and the Senate to agree that the amendment is necessary. The second way is for states to send **delegates** to a constitutional convention, where two-thirds of them must agree to propose the amendment. So far, the second method has never been used to add an amendment.

After amendments are proposed, they are sent to state **legislatures** to be **ratified.** To become law, amendments must be ratified by three-fourths of the states. Today, that means that 38 states must approve an amendment for it to become law.

Articles VI and VII and the Bill of Rights

Article VI of the Constitution says that the **debts** the United States had under the **Confederation** government continued under the new government. The article also mentions **treaties,** stating that any treaties made will become law, and that judges in every state must obey them. The article goes on to state that the members of the governmental branches are required to support the Constitution. However, they will never be asked to support any particular religion.

Article VII

This article refers to the **ratification** of the Constitution itself. It says that nine states must ratify the Constitution for it to become the governing document of the United States. In 1787 there were only thirteen states—so a two-third majority was nine states.

The **Bill of Rights** is an important addition to the U.S. Constitution. Many **delegates** to the Constitutional Convention argued for a bill of rights before they would ratify the Constitution.

On February 15, 2003, thousands of protesters gathered in New York City for an anti-war demonstration. The First Amendment of the Bill of Rights gives U.S. citizens the right to assemble. No one can tell another what he or she can or cannot protest against.

The Bill of Rights

Some states ratified the Constitution only after **Congress** promised to work on a bill of rights. So in 1789, Congress began drawing up a set of **amendments** that would become the Bill of Rights. The seventeen amendments were soon condensed to ten. In 1791, those ten amendments were ratified and added to the end of the Constitution.

The first ten amendments, or Bill of Rights, include rights and privileges of U.S. **citizens** that are *not* mentioned in the articles of the Constitution. The rights mentioned in the First Amendment include freedom of speech, freedom of the press, and freedom to assemble, or meet. The Bill of Rights also guarantees the right to bear arms—the right of citizens to own weapons, especially guns and other firearms. Other amendments describe the kind of trial a person who is accused of a crime can expect. The Ninth Amendment states that the rights listed above are not the only rights the people have. The Tenth Amendment says that any power not given to the United States by the Constitution, other than those powers that are against the law, are given to the individual states.

The Remaining Amendments

Between 1795 and 1992, seventeen other **amendments** were added to the Constitution. While all of the amendments are important, some are particularly notable because of their impact on United States society.

Amendment XV

The Fifteenth Amendment refers to the right to vote. This amendment was **ratified** in 1870, five years after slavery became illegal in the United States, and President Lincoln ordered that all slaves be freed (part of the Thirteenth Amendment). Slaves did not have the right to vote. Free African-American men, however, believed they should be allowed to vote, and this amendment guaranteed them that right. The wording of the amendment does not say just "men," though. It says "the right of **citizens** of the United States to vote shall not be denied" because of "race, color, or previous condition of **servitude**." The wording convinced many women that they, too, had the right to vote. After the Fifteenth Amendment was ratified, some women tried to vote but were stopped by officials.

The Eighteenth Amendment was widely ignored by most Americans. Here, an officer smashes a barrel of beer in 1924.

Amendment XVIII

In 1919, the Eighteenth Amendment was ratified and added to the Constitution. It made the manufacture, sale, and transportation of any alcoholic beverage illegal beginning in January 1920. The passage of this amendment began an era called

Prohibition, because liquor was **prohibited.** The amendment was **repealed** in 1933. The repeal of an amendment can only be done by adding another amendment that states that the previous one is repealed. In this case, the Twenty-first Amendment repealed the Eighteenth Amendment.

Amendment XIX

The Nineteenth Amendment, ratified in 1920, finally gave women the right to vote. For many years, women fought for this right, only to be continually denied. After a long battle, the right of women to vote was included in the Constitution.

Amendment XXVI

On July 1, 1971, the Twenty-sixth Amendment was ratified by **Congress.** This amendment gave citizens eighteen years of age and older the right to vote. It states, "the right of citizens of the United States, who are eighteen years of age or older, to vote shall not be denied . . ." This is one of the most recent amendments to the Constitution.

Amendments giving women the right to vote were presented to Congress for more than 40 years before the Nineteenth Amendment finally passed.

Travels of the Constitution

After the **engrossed** copy of the Constitution was presented to the Continental **Congress** in September 1787, it was kept in New York City, where Congress met. When George Washington became president in 1789, the Constitution and other important documents, including the **Declaration of Independence,** were given to the **secretary of state** for safekeeping. The first secretary of state was Thomas Jefferson.

In 1790, the U.S. government moved from New York City back to Philadelphia, Pennsylvania. In 1800, it moved to Washington, D.C., the new **federal** city that had been established as a home for the government. Until 1814, the Constitution was kept in the War Office building there.

Congress met in City Hall on Wall Street in New York City when the Constitution was written. For a while, the Constitution was stored there.

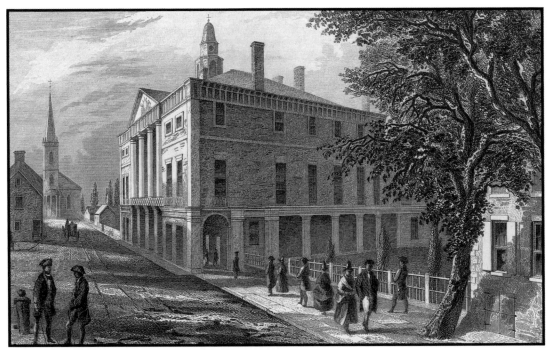

The War of 1812

As the British approached the nation's capital during the War of 1812, the Constitution and the Declaration of Independence, along with other important documents, were placed in sacks by then Secretary of State James Monroe. The documents were first stored in a barn in Virginia, then at the home of the Littlejohn family in Leesburg, Virginia. Monroe's move was a wise one because when the British entered Washington, D.C., they set fire to many buildings, including the White House.

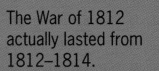

The British set fire to much of Washington, D.C., in 1812. The White House can be seen in the background in flames.

Hidden away

After the war, the Constitution was kept in a steel case by the various secretaries of state. It aged better than the Declaration of Independence, which was displayed for many years on a wall. The light from windows in the room contributed to the **deterioration** of the Declaration. The Constitution is in much better condition because it was not on display. Until the late 1800s, the document was not considered as important as the Declaration of Independence. In fact, no one thought much about the Constitution until 1885, when someone doing research in the State Department Library found it in the steel case at the bottom of a closet!

People from around the country came to the Library of Congress to view the Constitution and Declaration of Independence.

In 1920, the **secretary of state** decided that the documents kept in his care needed to be better preserved. The next year, he turned over the Constitution to the Library of Congress in Washington, D.C. There, the parchments were examined and **restored.** In 1924, the United States Constitution and **Declaration of Independence** were put into a fireproof display at the Library of Congress.

Stored in Fort Knox

During World War II, which took place from 1941 to 1945, the documents were moved because the government thought there could be an attack on the nation's capital. The Constitution was packed into a bronze container with a **lead** seal and taken to Fort Knox, Kentucky. There, it was placed in an underground vault. At Fort Knox, experts examined the document and made minor repairs to it.

At the Library of Congress

On October 1, 1944, the Constitution was returned to the Library of Congress and put into a **shrine** there, where it was on public display. The display was guarded at all times by a member of the U.S. military.

Moved to the NARA

In 1951, the head **archivist** at the National Archives, or NARA, decided it could provide a better home for the Constitution. On December 13, 1952, the Constitution and Declaration of Independence were transferred to the NARA. The documents were then put on display in the **rotunda** of the NARA building. The documents remained there until 1998. At that time, they were removed as the rotunda was being remodeled. The documents went back on display in late 2003.

There was a strong military presence when the Constitution was moved from the Library of Congress to the NARA.

The Constitution on Display

The new Charters of Freedom display, which opened in September 2003, placed the cases lower, so that children and people in wheelchairs could get a better view.

The exhibit at the NARA in Washington, D.C., is open to the public and includes not only the Constitution but the other documents in what are called the **Charters** of Freedom. Other documents on display are the **Declaration of Independence** and the **Bill of Rights.**

Keeping the documents safe

The Charters of Freedom are stored behind thick glass that contains a special filter so harmful rays of light cannot pass through. At night, a special machine lowers the documents into a vault that lies 22 feet (6.7 meters) below the exhibit hall. The vault weighs 55 tons (50 metric tons) and is made of steel and concrete. The vault is used to protect the documents and keep them safe.

In 1987, a three million dollar camera and a computer—that together make up the Charters Monitoring System—were purchased to check the documents regularly to make sure they remain in good condition. The system looks for flaking and fading ink, and it can tell if ink is rubbing onto the glass in front of the document. It takes one-inch (2.5-centimeter) photographs of the document from time to time, then checks each photograph to see if anything has changed.

Restoring the Constitution

In 1998, the public exhibit at the NARA closed so **conservators** could **restore** the documents. The Constitution was carefully removed from its case and closely checked for damage. The document was restored and put into a new case that was made using the best materials available. The case is made from a strong substance called titanium and is filled with a gas called argon to protect the ink. When the newly remodeled NARA **rotunda** reopened and the Charters of Freedom went back on display, all four pages of the Constitution were on view. Before, only pages one and four were shown.

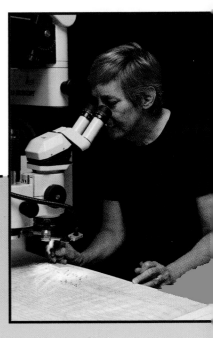

Conservator Catherine Nicholson uses a binocular microscope to examine the writing on the Constitution. She specifically check for flaking ink that needs to be reattached to the document.

Conserving the Constitution

When Mary Lynn Ritzenthaler and Catherine Nicholson, conservators at the NARA, opened the case that held the Constitution, they and their fellow conservators held their breath. No one had actually handled or examined the document since 1952. What would they find?

They discovered that the surface of the parchment was uneven and had what they call "hills and valleys." When they examined the document under a microscope, they saw that small flakes of ink had completely disappeared. Some flakes were still there, but were lifting off the parchment. Insects had eaten the edges of some of the pages, so they had a lacy appearance.

The conservators re-attached the ink flakes using a tiny watercolor brush and a substance made by cooking small scraps of parchment. Then they cleaned the document. Finally, they exposed the parchment to **humidity,** and re-stretched it to make it flatter.

A Living Document

The United States Constitution is probably one of the most important documents in the history of the nation. It not only provides a solid **foundation** for the government, but also guarantees certain rights to every American **citizen.**

The founders' intent

Having the original, signed copy of the Constitution means that no one can argue what the intent of the nation's founders was when they formed the government. We have their very words, in ink on parchment. We know what kind of government they wanted to form and what kind of nation they hoped would arise as time went on. And the idea that the signatures at the end of the document were written by the men who had a hand in creating the Constitution gives us a personal connection to them.

A firm base

In 1910, President William Howard Taft underlined the importance of the Constitution when he said that "[t]he **federal** Constitution has stood the test of more than a hundred years in supplying the powers that have been needed to make the Central Government as strong as it ought to be, and . . . I do not see why the Constitution may not serve our people always." Another president, Franklin D. Roosevelt, said in 1945 that "[o]ur Constitution . . . was not a perfect instrument, it is not perfect yet; but it provided a firm base upon which all manner of men of all races, colors and creeds [religions] could build our solid structure of democracy."

Franklin D. Roosevelt

The U.S. Constitution is not only important to Americans. It has influenced governments all over the world. In fact, its style and many of its ideas have been copied in later constitutions.

The Constitution lives on

Because the Constitution is so important, the preservation of the original document is critical. **Conservator** Catherine Nicholson said that:

> While some might argue that the Constitution is merely a musty document—old ink on old parchment—the ideas it contains continue to be argued and brought to bear on every aspect of American life. The concepts remain fresh and pertinent [relevant] to the latest-breaking news—to events that the Framers [writers] could not have imagined.

Children listen to a lecture on the Constitution at the NARA. This picture was taken before the new display opened in September 2003.

See the Constitution online

Go to http://www.archives.gov/exhibit_hall/charters_of_freedom/constitution/constitution.html to see the entire Constitution online.

Glossary

adjourn bring or come to a close, such as a meeting

adopt accept formally and put into effect

amendment change; in the Constitution, amendments are formal changes voted on by states

analyst person who closely examines something to determine whether it is real

archivist person responsible for keeping public records or historical documents

artifact object made and used by someone in the past

bill of rights document that lists the rights and privileges of all people in a nation

chairman person who leads a meeting or discussion

charter official document granting, guaranteeing, or showing the limits of the rights and duties of the group to which it is given.

chief justice head judge of a court

citizen person who lives in a city or town and owes loyalty to a government and is protected by it

commander-in-chief person who holds total control over the armed forces of a nation

compromise agreement that is the result of two sides giving up something

confederation agreement of support between political bodies

Congress formal meeting of delegates for discussion and usually action on some question; lawmaking body of the U.S. government

conservator person who is responsible for the care, restoration, and repair of documents and other historical artifacts

debate argument that follows certain rules

debt amount of money owed

Declaration of Independence document in which the American colonies formally declared independence from Great Britain in 1776

delegate person sent as a representative to a meeting or conference

deterioration wear and tear, become damaged in quality, condition, or value

draft prepare; unfinished form of a piece of writing

engross prepare the final handwritten or printed text of an official document

executive branch of government that carries out laws and includes the president

federal one central government that oversees smaller units; the smaller units, such as states, also have their own governments

federalist person who believes that one central government is better than many smaller governments

foundation support on which something rests, to create a new way of doing something

humidity amount of moisture, or water, in the air

journal written record of daily events

judicial branch of government that interprets the laws and includes the court system

lead soft metal

legislative branch of government that makes laws

legislature group of elected individuals who make laws for those who elect them

motion formal suggestion for action offered according to the rules of a meeting

pamphlet booklet with no cover, usually made of paper folded into smaller parts

parliamentary procedure specific way to hold meetings, based on certain orderly rules and systems

preamble introductory statement

primary source original copy of a journal, letter, newspaper, document, or image

prohibit not allowed

proportional representation system of government in which one person represents a certain number of people

pumice powdery substance made of glass from volcanoes

ratify vote to officially approve or accept

repeal overrule or dismiss; in Congress, to say "no" to an idea, proposal, or amendment

republican relating to a type of government in which power lies in the citizens through their right to vote

resolution formal statement of a belief or principle

restore put or bring back to an earlier or original state

revise make changes to

Revolutionary War American fight for independence from British rule between 1775–1783

rotunda round building covered by a dome; or large round room

secondary source written account of an event by someone who studied a primary source or sources

secretary of state person in the U.S. government who is responsible for foreign affairs

senator elected representative who serves in the Senate

servitude condition in which freedom is not given and in which one person serves another, such as slavery

shrine case or box for important artifacts or documents

stack structure of bookshelves for storing books, often used in libraries

Supreme Court highest court of the U.S. consisting of a chief justice and eight associate justices

term period of time fixed by law

treaty agreement, often between countries, arrived at after a negotiation process

union something, such as a nation, formed by combining parts or members

More Books to Read

Hossell, Karen Price. *The Bill of Rights.* Chicago: Heinemann Library, 2004.

Smolinski, Diane. *Important People of the Revolutionary War.* Chicago: Heinemann Library, 2002.

Stein, R. Conrad. *The National Archives.* Danbury, Conn.: Franklin Watts, 2002.

Index

DATE DUE

~~NOV 0 4 2005~~	
~~NOV 1 4 2006~~	
NOV 1 4 2005	